When RUTH BADER GINSBURG

Chewed 100 Sticks of Gum

by Mark Weakland   illustrated by Daniela Volpari

PICTURE WINDOW BOOKS
a capstone imprint

Ruth Bader Ginsburg placed her left hand on the Bible. Next, she raised her right hand. She swore to uphold the law. Then she smiled. The audience, including the President of the United States, applauded. She was now a justice of the United States Supreme Court.

Ruth was the first female Jewish American to sit on the court. She was also only the second woman to do so. She got there through study and hard work. And she knew that girls would follow in her footsteps.

"One day there will be as many women as men sitting as judges in our country," she said.

Joan Ruth Bader was born on March 15, 1933. Her parents, Nathan and Celia Bader, were Jewish immigrants from Russia. They had little money. The family rented the first floor of a small house in New York City.

Baby Joan had one sister, Marilyn. Marilyn loved little Ruth. She tickled her belly. She made her yell and kick. "You're such a kicky baby," she said. "We're going to call you Kiki."

Later, Joan would go by her middle name. There were several other Joans in her kindergarten class — but no other Ruths.

Sadly, Marilyn and Ruth did not have much time together.
Marilyn died when Ruth was 14 months old.

The death of her daughter broke Celia Bader's heart. But she
never stopped thinking about Ruth's future. She swore that
Ruth would have a life different from hers.

Celia had not gone to college. Her parents could only afford
to send one child to college. They had sent her brother.

Celia wanted Ruth to do well in school so she could grow into an independent adult. She did not want Ruth to grow up to rely on a man. What did Ruth want? She wanted to make her mother happy. She worked hard to always get good grades.

Ruth was left-handed. A teacher tried to make her write with her other hand. But writing with her right hand was unnatural, so Ruth got a D in penmanship.

"I'm never writing with my right hand again!" she said.

Do you know what happened? Ruth never did. And she never got another D in school.

9

Ruth's parents worked hard. They wanted to give their daughter a bright future. Nathan sold furs and hats. Celia stayed at home to care for Ruth. She was careful with their funds. Any extra money was saved for Ruth's college education.

Ruth went shopping with her mother every day. While they ran errands, Celia gave her advice. She encouraged Ruth to think clearly. She told her to be true to herself. These talks made an impression on Ruth.

"I love you, mama," she said. **"You're the bravest and strongest person I know."**

CANDY

Ruth's mother was a wonderful role model. But Ruth also often found strong female role models in the books she read. Ruth loved to read about Amelia Earhart. A real-life pilot, Amelia was the first woman to fly across the Atlantic Ocean.

Nancy Drew was another favorite. Nancy was a detective who solved mysteries.

"Kiki, why do you love Nancy so much?" asked her mother. "She isn't even real."

Nancy was **"an adventurer, who could think for herself,"** Ruth answered.

Ruth loved storytelling too. She entertained her cousins with dramas she made up. She also read poetry out loud. One of her favorites was "The Jabberwocky," by Lewis Carroll. Another was the poem written on the base of the Statue of Liberty. Ruth knew all the words. "Give me your tired, your poor, your huddled masses yearning to breathe free."

Ruth also liked the outdoors. All the kids in her Brooklyn neighborhood played on the street. They ran, roller-skated, and jumped rope. The fun lasted until dark.

Ruth's best friend was a girl named Marilyn. She invited Ruth to join her family for dinner. The food was often spaghetti and meatballs. At Ruth's house, the girls played jacks on the front steps.

Life in the city was not all fun and games. Ruth grew up when America was at war. By 1944, air raid drills were just part of the school day. When sirens shrieked, students took shelter.

Ruth and her classmates helped the war effort. They grew vegetables in a victory garden to give out to people during the war. They also chewed hundreds of sticks of gum. What did this have to do with helping? The gum was wrapped in aluminum foil. Students rolled the silver wrappers into balls. The balls were sent to a factory that made parts for airplanes.

In addition to helping the war effort, Ruth started to notice some things about her world. She saw that some people were treated unfairly. Jewish boys were allowed to do more than Jewish girls. But most Jewish people were discriminated against. Many Jews, including Ruth's family, immigrated to America before the war. They had hoped to escape violence

Once, while driving past a resort, Ruth saw a disturbing sign. "Look, Mama! It says, 'No dogs or Jews allowed.' Doesn't that make you angry?"

Her mother shook her head. "Getting angry is a waste of time, Kiki."

Because of moments like these, Ruth learned how to let go of anger and move on.

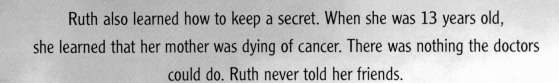

Ruth also learned how to keep a secret. When she was 13 years old, she learned that her mother was dying of cancer. There was nothing the doctors could do. Ruth never told her friends.

Writing helped Ruth keep her mind off her mother's illness. She worked on the school newspaper. She was also the editor. Other students wrote about things like the school play and the circus. But Ruth enjoyed writing about the Bill of Rights and the Ten Commandments.

281 – 310>

At Madison High School, Ruth was known as a quiet but popular girl. She continued to write and work on the newspaper. She played the cello. And she was a member of the Honor Society.

Ruth also belonged to the Go-Getters. It was a pep club for sporting and social events. Members wore black satin jackets. She sold tickets to football games. She twirled a baton. Once, she lost control of it. The flying baton chipped her tooth. Ouch!

Ruth's greatest sorrow was losing her mother. Celia died the day before Ruth's high school graduation. Ruth did not go to her graduation ceremony. But she knew she had made her mother proud. She won medals. She earned scholarships. And she was going to Cornell University, one of the best colleges in the country.

"Mother wanted me to study hard and get good grades and succeed in life," Ruth told a friend. So that's what she did.

Afterword

In the 1950s, Ruth met and married her Cornell University classmate, Martin Ginsburg. Ruth loved that he was interested in her ideas and thoughts. They were both accepted to Harvard Law School. But Martin was drafted into the military. Then he developed a terrible form of cancer. Ruth cared for him, their young daughter, and took law school classes. She had to fight discrimination, in both the classroom and as a lawyer. Not everyone thought a woman — and a Jewish woman at that — could be a good teacher or lawyer. But in the end, she triumphed. Martin survived, and her family thrived.

Ruth graduated first in her law school class. Then she became a respected university professor. In 1980, she became a judge. And in 1993, she was named a Supreme Court Justice. As a member of the court, she ruled on many historic cases. In 2015, she and five other justices upheld a law that changed America's health care system. That same year, she and four others ruled that people in all 50 states were allowed to marry whomever they wanted.

Throughout her career, Ruth has spoken in favor of keeping religion and government apart. She has supported the rights of workers. And she has ruled to treat people equally.

"I try to teach through my opinions, through my speeches, how wrong it is to judge people on the basis of what they look like, color of their skin, whether they're men or women."

Glossary

afford — have enough money to pay for

baton — a long stick with rubber ends that can be twirled

discrimination — unjust treatment of certain people

drama — a play with great emotion

errand — a short journey to deliver or collect something

immigrant — a person who comes to live permanently in a foreign country

independent — not relying on something or someone else

justice — a judge of the supreme court of a country or state

satin — smooth, glossy fabric usually made of silk

shriek — a high-pitched cry or yell

Read More

Levy, Debbie. *I Dissent: Ruth Bader Ginsburg Makes Her Mark.* New York: Simon & Schuster Books for Young Readers, 2016.

Stoltman, Joan. *20 Fun Facts About the Supreme Court.* Fun Fact File: US History! New York: Gareth Stevens Publishing, 2018.

Winter, Jonah. *Ruth Bader Ginsburg: The Case of R.B.G. Vs. Inequality.* New York: Abrams Books for Young Readers, 2018.

Critical Thinking Questions

1. What character traits and abilities did Ruth Bader Ginsburg have as a child that helped her become a Justice of the United States Supreme Court?

2. Find two websites that list the current Supreme Court justices of the United States. Make a list of the Justices. What are their names? How long have they served? How many of them are women and how many are men?

3. Identify two ideas or thoughts Ruth believed to be important. Then tell why you chose these two thoughts or ideas. Use evidence from the text to support your reasoning.

Index

Internet Sites

FactHound offers a safe, fun way to find Internet sites related to this book. All of the sites on FactHound have been researched by our staff.

Here's all you do:

Visit *www.facthound.com*

Type in this code: 9781515830399

Other Titles in this Series

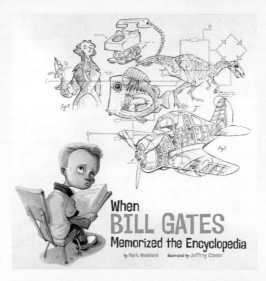

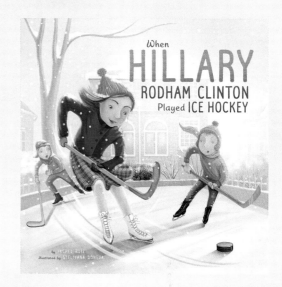

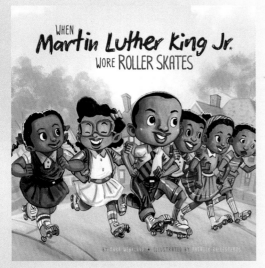

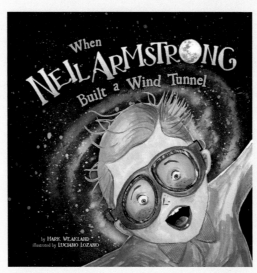

Special thanks to our adviser for his advice and expertise:
James N. Druckman PhD, Northwestern University, Evanston, Illinois
Department of Political Science

Editor: Mari Bolte
Designer: Ashlee Suker
Creative Director: Nathan Gassman
Production Specialist: Kris Wilfahrt
The illustrations in this book were created digitally.

Editor's Note: Direct quotations are indicated by **bold** words.

Direct quotations are found on the following pages:

page 2, line 8: Biskupic, Joan.
"Ginsburg Sworn In as 107th Justice and 2nd Woman on Supreme Court," The Washington Post.
http://www.washingtonpost.com/wp-dyn/content/article/2007/08/23/AR2007082300968.html

page 11, line 4: Ginsburg, Ruth.
My Own Words. New York: Simon & Schuster, 2016, page 196.

page 13, line 3: Carmon, Irin.
Notorious RBG: The Life and Times of Ruth Bader Ginsburg. New York: Harper,
an imprint of HarperCollins Publishers, 2017, page 29.

page 26, line 5, Ibid., page 31

page 28, line 14: "Ruth Bader Ginsburg Biography." The Biography.com website.
https://www.biography.com/people/ruth-bader-ginsburg-9312041

Picture Window Books are published by Capstone,
1710 Roe Crest Drive, North Mankato, Minnesota 56003
www.mycapstone.com

Library of Congress Cataloging-in-Publication Data
Names: Weakland, Mark, author. | Volpari, Daniela, 1985– illustrator.
Title: When Ruth Bader Ginsburg chewed 100 sticks of gum / by Mark Weakland ; illustrated by Daniela Volpari.
Description: North Mankato, Minnesota : Picture Window Books, [2018]
Identifiers: LCCN 2018018822 (print) | LCCN 2018019082 (ebook) | ISBN 9781515830528 (eBook PDF) |
ISBN 9781515830399 (library binding) | ISBN 9781515830481 (paperback)
Subjects: LCSH: Ginsburg, Ruth Bader—Juvenile literature. | Women judges—United States—Biography—Juvenile
literature. | Jewish judges—United States—Biography—Juvenile literature. | Judges—United States—Biography—
Juvenile literature. | United States. Supreme Court—Biography—Juvenile literature. | Illustrated children's books.
Classification: LCC KF8745.G56 (ebook) | LCC KF8745.G56 W43 2018 (print) | DDC 347.73/2634 [B]—dc23
LC record available at https://lccn.loc.gov/2018018822

Printed in the United States   4474